Planet Earth. Early 21st Century.

地球，二十一世纪初。

致力于纪念黄帝

HUANGDI
in memoriam

黄宝书
THE LITTLE YELLOW BOOK

习大大主席语录
QUOTATIONS FROM CHAIRMAN XI DADA

[CURATED BY JULIE O'YANG]

ˊ　ˊ　｜　ˋ　ˋ

UNABRIDGED
UNAUTHORIZED
VERSION

Don't believe the hype. Don't, don't, don't.
Public Enemy, 1988

Only socialism can save China.
只有社会主义才能救中国。

Xi Jinping
习近平

Socialism requires a lot of work.

社会主义是干出来的。

Xi Jinping

习近平

WHO IS XI DADA?

'Dada' literally translates into "big big", meaning father in rural Northwest China where Xi Jinping hails from. It's the CCP's propaganda machine spinning a "love and fondness" brand for Xi, denoting a glowing, fatherly figure with nothing but his 1.3 billion children's interest at heart.

On a mission to bring the most powerful man in China closer to the people as well as to make a business from it, a 29-year-old former deliveryman Zhang Hongming (张洪明) began a series of experiment through his Weibo, the Chinese equivalent of Twitter. Until recently, reporting on national leaders - let alone making money in the process - was considered the exclusive province of official media like China Central Television (CCTV).

For his online shop named Study Xi Fan Club, Zhang wanted to find a name that showed a softer side of Xi Jinping, whose official titles bristle with authority: President, General Secretary of the Communist Party and Chairman of the Central Military Commission. But nothing stuck until late-2012 when he posted a picture of Xi crouching to pick up a dart as part of a Maori ceremony in Auckland. *"Xi Dada, what are you about to do here?"* the self-employed microblogger wrote. Zhang didn't know it then that Xi Dada would become a key element of a personality promotion campaign to buff the image of a man whose terrific centralization of power has earned him comparisons to Chairman Mao.

Xinhua, the Chinese state-run news agency, called the president "*a tough man with a tender heart*". The People's Daily used Xi Dada twenty one times in a single article, and followed that with an online propaganda video that began: "*In China, we call him Xi Dada*". Aside from being the strong leader, Xi turns out to be an ideal Chinese husband as well. "*If you want to marry, marry someone like Xi Dada, a man full of heroism with an unyielding spirit; no matter how the world changes and how many difficulties lie ahead, he will insist and keep moving forward,*" sung the lyrics to a song that has gone viral on the internet in the mainland.

here on youtube > *bit.ly/XiDada*

FOREWORD TO THE FIRST EDITION
OF "QUOTATIONS FROM CHAIRMAN XI DADA"
(Fall of 2018)

The purpose of this book is to distill the huge volumes of Xi Jinping Thought and pen it into a small booklet that even a semi-illiterate could read, memorize, or set to music. Like its famous predecessor, the Little Red Book[1], the quotes are plucked out of context and strung together without much regard for chronology.

We all know the Little Red Book, which apparently has inspired our Little Yellow Book. The former was used during the Cultural Revolution not only simply to streamline ideology, but also as a weapon to defend China against its enemies from inside and outside of the socialist country.

Ours is an attempt to run through the instructions of China's current leader on a variety of wide-ranging subjects, from culture and art to climate change, from Internet to economy to military strategy and national security, within a limited number of easy-to-read pages. While currently being fleshed out by Party scholars, "Xi Jinping Thought on Socialism with Chinese Characteristic for a New Era" is commanding domestic media channels as well as occupying the country's ad spaces and billboards to be studied on a daily basis by its citizens. School children and

Party officials alike have been learning the theories named after political theorists like Karl Marx, Vladimir Lenin and Mao Zedong. Several universities decided to teach the President's philosophy[2]; college students and white-collar employees receive certificates for accurately memorizing Xi Jinping Thought and use it as a guidebook for living, working and policymaking. In the first week of October 2018, Hunan TV, one of China's largest television networks, has aired a new quiz show about the life and philosophy of China's current leader. The ideology was recently written into the Chinese Constitution.

With the rise of China as an economic wunderkind, Mr. Xi's aphorisms have become so common that they are cited and referred to on international media channels as well. Just like Chairman Mao Thought that reflected a unique time period in human history, Xi Jinping's sayings capture a high spot of our global world and hold significant historical value. And just like Chairman Mao, president Xi Jinping, the head of China's ruling party, state and military - and who is now widely seen as the most powerful leader in decades, aims to transform China into a modern country that leads the world's agriculture, industry, science and military and defense. This is Mr. Xi's Chinese Dream.

On March 11 2018, the National People's Congress passed the historic constitutional amendments with 2,958 votes in favor of removing presidential term limits[3].To further assert the party's supremacy over the state, the constitution now declares the Party's leadership as the *"most fundamental feature of socialism with Chinese characteristics".*

Despite Mr. Xi's enthusiasm for status, what are the essentials of the Chinese Dream he designed for his country and nation exactly?

Why does his dream make China tick?

There are three mainstays.

To begin with, China is a Marxist entrepreneur. The term rather gives away the nature of Chinese Marxism.

Remember when you started to touch the subject "China" for the first time and how people couldn't wait to recommend you "Four Books and Five Classics"? And a day is not lived if Confucius' name is not readily dropped?

On September 24 2014, something significant took place that escaped the attention of the world. China's president Xi Jinping attended the ostentatious celebration of Confucius' 2565th birthday and delivered a speech. This was the first time that the head of state ever took part in such an event. The Chinese Communist party became an official fan, nearly half a century after Chairman Mao ordered "Annihilating the Confucius' Family Business" [4].

"Confucianism reflects the spiritual pursuit of the Chinese nation, the essential nourishment for the continuous growth and advancement of the Chinese nation," Xi pronounced imperatively making Confucian ideals a required part of his Chinese Dream and the basics of Rejuvenation of the Chinese Nation. President Xi quotes Confucian classics in his countless speeches dominating official news channels and has transformed himself

into a faithful successor of Confucian tradition.

But what did the Master comment on "strong man politics"? In Analects[5] Confucius replied to the question if there is one single phrase that might ruin a country: *"I do not have an answer. However I do hear people say that the pleasure of being a ruler is no-one dares to defy my words. If they are correct words, why should it not be a good thing? However, if they are incorrect words and yet no-one dare to disagree with him, then perhaps he could destroy the country with one single utterance!"*

The Chinese authorities encourage private schools to teach Confucian piety and obedience. College students wear modern imitation of Confucian scholar costumes at graduation ceremonies and young female students even volunteer to demonstrate bound feet experiments on campuses[6]. As of October 2017, a total of 516 Confucius Institutes and 1,076 Confucius Classrooms have been established in 142 countries and regions, according to the Confucius Institute Headquarters. Among them, 135 Confucius Institutes were set up in 51 countries along the Belt and Road. The government aims to establish 1,000 Confucius Institutes by 2020.

While the ancient -isms are admirable without doubt, they may not provide the key to understand modern China. The ancient tomes have served and continue to serve as a nifty marketing tool; a brand name to convince the foreigners as well as to influence China's rising middle class. It's stunningly successful PR from the Chinese Communist Party.

So what is Chinese Marxism, popularly known

as "socialism with Chinese characteristics"? Socialism with Chinese characteristics is something that combines the basic principles of scientific socialism with the facts of building socialism unique to China. Socialism is the common rule and essential feature of the practice, while Chinese characteristics are what the basic principles of socialism really embody in China[7].

China's effort to uphold socialism is sincere, and even more heartfelt than the ruling party's steamy but fairly opportunistic, or pragmatic, fling with Confucianism. This is vital to understand today's China in all its complexity and apparent paradoxes. China clearly sees itself as a socialist country and believes in its cause to the eternal happy end, and for this reason it will never sign up to the capitalist West.

Nevertheless, if Marxism is a distinct discipline in China, what about Mao Zedong Thought that has translated the foreign sounds into something with Chinese characteristics? The second mainstay of the Chinese Dream, Mao Zedong Thought remains the focus of intense study and debate in China – so much so that Xi Jinping repeatedly quotes Mao in national and international contexts[8]. Xi has a PhD in Marxism and has directed even more resources to the study and fostering of the Marxist tradition and the work of Mao Zedong. All this makes sense to him, even though it may seem less coherent to an outsider. Mao's legacy is alive and kicking despite his controversial project, the Cultural Revolution, which is still a delicate subject matter under the current government.

The third mainstay is nationalism[9]. Since his

appointment, Xi has worked assiduously to neutralize rivals and potential enemies as well as overseen the construction of a highly sophisticated authoritarian state. Coupled with this is a vigorously promoted vision of China as a global superpower. His Chinese dream captures a new, muscular iteration of China's self-narrative that demands verbal space. *"We have yellow skin and black hair. We are called the descendants of the dragon,"* he articulated during president Trump's visit to China in November 2017.

[The Curatorship]

NOTES TO THE FOREWORD

1 In 2013, China launched a campaign to reprint and revamp Chairman's Mao's Quotations, "the world's second most published book" after the Bible.

2 "Xi Jinping Thought to be taught in China's universities"
Here on the The Guardian > bit.ly/XiThoughtU

3 Before 1978 it was common for a high-ranking Party official to hold a corresponding executive position in the government and/or military. It was Deng Xiaoping, the Party paramount leader, who pronounced "socialism with Chinese characteristics" for the first time, took the initiative aiming at reducing dramatically the multiple hat wearing of office holders. In a speech "On the reform of the system of party and state leadership" delivered on August 18, 1980, Deng said: "First of all, it is not good to have an over-concentration of power. It hinders the practice of socialist democracy and of the Party's democratic centralism, impedes the progress of socialist construction and prevents us from taking full advantage of collective wisdom." Recently, Chinese president Xi Jinping expressed his views that he is "personally opposed" to life-long rule. The official proposal to drop term limit already came in February, three weeks before the final tally of the vote that allows Xi to be president for life.

Here on Financial Times > bit.ly/XinotforLife

4 In November 1966, Mao-supporting Red Guards gathered in Beijing's Tiananmen Square and swore to *"annihilate the Kong family business."* A few days later, they descended on Confucius' hometown Qufu, where they smashed statues of Confucius as well as commemorative stele in the temple and the family mansion. Then, with the help of local workers, the Red Guards began a frenzy of destruction in the Kong family cemetery. The youths dug up over 2,000 graves, looted their contents, and hung the naked corpses from trees. A remarkable quote attributed to Mao has been circulating around the Chinese Internet in recent years:

"We communists have started from criticizing Confucius. However, we must not go back to the closed path and give him our approval again. If we use Confucian thoughts to educate the common people with the intention of consolidating our power, we will fall into the historical recycle. This is not right. If the Communist Party can no longer rule and has to invite Confucius back into our policies, it means you are almost finished."

Read more here > bit.ly/NoConfucius

5 Original quote from Confucius' "Analects"

曰："一言而丧邦，有诸？"孔子对曰："言不可以若是其几也。人之言曰：'予无乐乎为君，唯其言而莫予违也。'如其善而莫之违也，不亦善乎？如不善而莫之违也，不几乎一言而

6 Foot-binding is said to have been inspired by a 10th-century court dancer named Yao Niang who bound her feet into the shape of a new moon. She entranced the emperor with a special dance inside a six-foot golden lotus. Walking on her crescent feet, she also invented the fashionable "willow gait", a sort Monroe movement. The practice was gradually adopted by elite women, making it a status symbol. The most desirable bride possessed a three-inch foot, known as a "golden lotus". Neo-Confucianism in Song era (960-1279) was the closest China had to a state religion. Neo-Confucianists placed extra emphasis on chastity and obedience for women. A good wife exists to serve her husband, to produce a son, to subjugate herself to in-laws and she must never remarry if widowed. The pain involved in foot-binding and the physical limitations it created became her demonstration of commitment to Confucian values. Under the Mongol rule (1271-1368), foot-binding became an expression of cultural identity. The cruel practice was proof of Chinese cultural superiority to the barbarians who ruled them. A woman's virtues were squeezed into one single act. Foot-binding was banned in 1912, although the practice lasted long into 1930's. The last factory making lotus shoes closed in 1999.

For the past 5-6 years, "traditional feminine virtue" schools have popped up across China. The schools aim to coach modern women to become obedient wives and daughter-in-laws, preaching values and visions such as "a disobedient woman is prone to cancer and all kinds of deadly diseases. In the past, women didn't have these diseases because in the past even women were beaten during the day, she obeyed in the evening", or "a woman who orders takeaway meals to avoid dish washing is a woman who doesn't abide by ancient virtues". These trendy schools are well-liked by unban professional women and university students seeking female identity. With this group, foot-binding has also become a status symbol, as the used tools and shoes are mainly antiques.

Some extra information (Chinese Only)
"To restore traditional culture, some feminine virtues schools become obsessed with footbinding" > *bit.ly/BindingSchool*
A university student records her experiences and observation at a feminine virtues school > *bit.ly/VirtuesInsider*
A tweet on a footbinding gallery, in the meantime censored.
> *bit.ly/HellenWang*

[7] "Socialism with Chinese Characteristics" (official definition) People's Daily reporting on the 17th National Congress of the Communist Party of China (NCCPC)
here > *bit.ly/ChinCharac*

[8] "Is Xi or isn't Xi? Quiz: who said it - Xi Jinping or Mao Zedong?" The Guardian, 24 October 2017
here > *bit.ly/XiorMaoQuiz*

[9] For historical reasons, Chinese nationalism is in many ways specific and expresses China's core interest in different periods of time. In 1905 **Sun Yat-sen** (1867-1925), the founding father of the modern Chinese nation announced his Three Principles of the People, a political philosophy developed by Sun as part of a philosophy to make China a free,

prosperous, and powerful nation. The three principles are **nationalism**, **democracy**, and the **livelihood of the people**. Sun Yat-sen's nationalism emphasizes especially Han Chinese nationalism, including independence from imperialist domination and taking back power from the foreign Manchu, the Qing dynasty. During Confucius' 2565th anniversary, Xi spoke to the guests: *"From Confucius to Sun Yat-sen, we all make sure that we draw beneficial nutrients from their legacy."*

CONTENTS

I

CHINESE DREAM

到2049 年新中国成立100年
时建成富强民主文明和谐的社会主义现代化国家。
By 2049, with the 100th anniversary of New China
(PRC) upon us, our country will become a
prosperous, strong, democratic, civilized,
harmonious, socialist, modern society.

Achieving the rejuvenation of our nation will be no walk in the park, and it will take more than drum beating and gong striking to get there.

The Chinese Dream is also a dream of cooperation, development, peace and mutual benefit, and it is akin to the American Dream.

This dream is about building a strong nation. For our armed forces, this dream is about building a strong army.

After making a good start, we should ensure that the cause achieves fruition. The great rejuvenation of the Chinese nation requires the dedicated effort of one generation after another. Having created a splendid civilization of over 5,000 years, the Chinese nation will certainly usher in an even more splendid future.

Without legacy and advancement of our civilization, without glory and triumph of our culture, we can't make Chinese Dream successful.

I believe that the great rejuvenation of the

Chinese nation is the country's greatest dream in modern times.

We have proposed the two centenary goals, i.e. to double the 2010 GDP and per capita income of every Chinese and complete the building of a moderately prosperous society by 2020 and to build a prosperous, strong, democratic, culturally advanced and harmonious modern socialist country and realize the great rejuvenation of the Chinese nation by the middle of the century. Whatever we do now is aimed at fulfilling these goals.

The prosperity of a country and nation is always supported by cultural prosperity. Without the legacy of the Chinese civilization and the improvement of it, without promoting and backing our culture, it's impossible to fulfill the Chinese Dream.

The Chinese people living in our great motherland during our great times share the opportunity to win and make our dreams come true. We enjoy the opportunity to grow and progress together with our motherland and our times. We have dreams and opportunities. We make a great effort. It is possible for us to create glorious things. The Chinese people of all nationalities must remember their mission and remain closely united in mind and strength so that we can bring together the wisdom and determination of one billion Chinese people that is of an invincible, majestic force.

The essence of soccer is not only about athletics, but it is also to enhance the people's physique, to cultivate patriotism, collectivism and the tenacious fighting spirit. If we choose the right path, we are not afraid it's going to be a long journey. We are determined to achieve the Chinese "Soccer Dream".

II

SOCIALISM
WITH CHINESE
CHARACTERISTICS

毛泽东思想和中国特色社会主义理论体系作为马克思主义中
国化的理论成果，内蕴着丰富的优秀传统文化。
Mao Zedong Thought and socialism with Chinese
characteristics are both the theoretical outcome of
the China-ization of Marxism and both hold the rich
foundations of the outstanding Chinese tradition.

Marxism-Leninism and Mao Zedong Thought must not be abandoned or else we lose our roots.

First of all, we must conscientiously study Marxist theory. This is a housekeeping skill for all our work. It is also a master skill that our leading cadres must have that will guarantee our success.

Socialism with Chinese characteristics entering a new era means that scientific socialism is full of vitality in 21st century China, and that the banner of socialism with Chinese characteristics is now flying high and proud for all to see.

Stand by and cultivate socialism with Chinese characteristics is like writing a big article. And now the task for our generation of Communists is to continue writing this big article.

The leadership of the Chinese Communist Party is the most essential feature of socialism with Chinese characteristics and the greatest advantage of the socialist system with Chinese characteristics.

Our Party has the historical mission of leading

the people of all nationalities to achieve the Two Centenary Goals and realize the great rejuvenation of the Chinese nation. At the same time, we also face the Four Trials and Four Dangers. To complete the historical mission and overcome the uncompromising challenges, we must control the Party and rule the Party so that we can ensure that the Party always stays the strong heart of the core leadership of socialism with Chinese characteristics.

It makes clear that the defining feature of socialism with Chinese characteristics is the leadership of the Communist Party of China. The greatest strength of the system of socialism with Chinese characteristics is the leadership of the Communist Party of China. The Party is the highest force for political leadership.

Going forward, under the leadership of the Communist Party of China, we, people of all ethnicities across the country, should take Marxism-Leninism, Mao Zedong Thought, Deng Xiaoping Theory, the important thought of Three Represents and the Scientific Outlook on Development as our guide to action. We should follow the path of socialism with Chinese characteristics, pursue the Four-pronged Comprehensive Strategy, promote patriotism and the great spirit of resisting aggression and forge ahead as one to reach our goals.

It is an important mission of our Party to eliminate poverty, improve the people's livelihood and gradually realize common prosperity. It is the essential requirement of socialism. China, meanwhile, has become the country with the most successful poverty reduction program in the world and has achieved the UN Millennium Development Goals as the first country. This accomplishment is enough to be written into human history. It proves to the world the superiority of the leadership of the Chinese Communist Party and the superiority of socialism with Chinese characteristics.

Not only must we finish building a moderately prosperous society in all respects and achieve the first centenary goal; we must also draw on this success to embark on a new journey toward the second centenary goal of fully building a modern socialist country.

With decades of hard work, socialism with Chinese characteristics has crossed the threshold into a new era.

III

COMMUNIST PARTY

党政军民学，东西南北中，党是领导一切的。[1] Governme
nt, the military, society and schools, north, south,
east and west
– the party leads them all.[1]

1 [This quote is originally from Mao Zedong's speech during the Politburo meeting in December 1973.President Xi reused the quote, which the 19th Party Congress agreed to enshrine this political principle into the Party constitution.]

Let our Party never be corrupted and the red color of our country never be polluted.

The purpose for our Party to lead our people to carry out the revolutionary and constructive reform is to make the Chinese people become prosperous, to make our country strong up, to rejuvenate the great Chinese nation.

The Communist Party of China is the biggest political party in the world. We must live up to our reputation.

The Party's ability to innovate, power to unite, and energy to fight have all been significantly strengthened, and the Party's engagement with the people has been greatly improved.

Some cadres avoid facing major issues and don't dare to be themselves. They are defensive and are afraid of losing a rating. They are afraid that people would say that they are not open-minded and liberal. This is absolutely wrong! Where does this vanity come from? What kind of an image do they want to have? They clearly pretend to be open-minded! We should remember there are no enlightened gentlemen on the battlefield. There are no enlightened gentlemen when facing major issues either and we must fight right and wrong. We cadres do not think about receiving encouragement from various people and winning praise from overseas public opinion.

We must dare to rule, dare to be in charge and dare to dazzle the enemy's eye with our sword.

Our ideological work means to consolidate the guiding position of Marxism in the field of ideology. All propaganda and ideological departments, every party member and cadre on the ideological front should clearly advocate the principle of the Party.

Adhering to the leadership of the Communist Party of China is not about not wanting democracy. It is about forming a broader and more effective democracy. We should not forget our aspiration for the multiple party cooperation and keep paving the road to the political development of socialism with Chinese characteristics. We must uphold, develop, and improve our country's socialist party system.

Our ideals and principles are like "calcium" for every Communist Party member. If we cease to have our ideals and principles, if they are not firm, it will cause spiritual "calcium deficiency" and we will be ill.

The original aspiration and mission of the Chinese Communists is to seek happiness for our people as well as to realize the rejuvenation of our nation.

Our Party should always be one with the people in heart and soul.

As long as our Party stays competent and strong and as long as we always remain true to the people's aspiration and work in concert with the people, we can and will navigate the great ship carrying the great dream of the Chinese people to break the waves and reach our glorious destination! [2]

2 [In the early 20th century, the Chinese intellectuals embarked on a peculiar journey of reinventing Chinese religions, which was an attempted fusion of different religions, cultures, or philosophies. The tendency to incorporate most of the religious traditions existing in China

Practice has proven that our Party is a Party that pursues a scientific approach with outspoken progressive methods. Our Party has survived all kinds of perils and has continuously grown to be mature and confident. Our Party has always been the core force to lead the people of all nationalities to sustain and improve socialism with Chinese characteristics.

Why must we unwaveringly assert our party's control over the military? Because this is the lesson the Soviet collapse teaches. The Soviet Red Army was depoliticized and departyized, becoming a national institution, and so the Soviet Communist

Party surrendered its weapons.

Fight to win! Forge exemplary conduct! Always listen to and follow the Party's orders, and march to wherever the Party points.

In order to uphold and develop socialism with Chinese characteristics in the new era, our party must have the courage to carry out self-reform to make the Party stronger.

In the end, Gorbachev only said a few words and announced the ending of the Soviet Communist Party. A big party was gone just like that. Proportionally, the Soviet Communist Party had more members than we (Communist Party of China) do, but nobody was man enough to say no.

IV

CONFUCIANISM

儒家思想反映了中华民族的精神追求，
是中华民族生生不息、发展壮大的重要滋养。

Confucianism reflects the spiritual pursuit of the
Chinese nation. It is the essential nourishment for
the continuous growth and advancement of the
Chinese nation.

Chinese Communists have always been loyal successors and promoters of China's outstanding tradition. From Confucius to Sun Yat-sen, we all make sure that we draw beneficial nutrients from their legacy.

The Chinese have a long tradition and therefore we surely are able to create the new wonder of the Chinese culture. To study Confucius and Confucianism, we must maintain a historical materialist view, turn the ancient understanding for our present use and filter the essence as well as sift the truth. In this way we can not only make the best use of it, but we can also deepen our examination so that it continues to play an active role under the new conditions of our times.

The outstanding Chinese tradition, such as Confucianism contains important clues for solving the problems that contemporary humankind is facing.

V

MY COUNTRY, MY PEOPLE

黑头发、黄皮肤，我们叫龙 [3] 的传人。

We have black hair and yellow skin. We are called
the descendants of the dragon.[3]

3 [In 1644, the Manchus, a nomadic group that came from the north overthrew China's Ming dynasty and established Qing dynasty that ruled the empire until 1911. Manchu emperors not only had borrowed Chinese administration and government structure and integrated their own bannermen system with it, but they had also taken and used symbols from traditional Chinese mythology, most notably the dragon. Before Qing dynasty, the dragon was only associated with the supreme ruler. It was the Manchus who popularized the dragon as the nation's cultural icon. The flag of Qing dynasty from the late 19th century featured the Azure Dragon on a plain yellow field with the red flaming pearl in the upper left corner. It became the first national flag of China.]

The Chinese character Ren or people is in a shape of two strokes supporting each other.

The Chinese people are a great people; they are industrious and brave and they never pause in pursuit of progress.

I want to press the "like" button for our great Chinese people.

I applaud the Chinese people for their great creativity.

We, the new generation, should accomplish our new Long March.

The future of China belongs to the people with positive knowledge and positive mind; the people who spread positive energy. The real crisis is not the financial crisis but a crisis of morality and faith. The bigger one's blessing, the bigger his field. Team up with wise people and good, kind colleagues. Bear common people in your heart; remarkable love conquers all.

Our Fitness for All Initiative is a national wellbeing plan. We want the Chinese people to enjoy a longer life expectancy and better health.

The Chinese nation is a great nation; it has been through hardships and adversity but remains indomitable.

Empty talks can waste a great country, while hard work can launch a great nation.

The Chinese nation, which since modern times began has endured so much for so long, has achieved a tremendous transformation. It has stood up, grown rich, and become strong, and it now embraces the brilliant prospects of rejuvenation.

I believe, as long as 1.3 billion people can keep the great innovative spirit (like in ancient times), we can create miracles one after another.

People are the real heroes.

The greatest contribution to the whole of human race, made by China, is to prevent its 1.3 billion people from hunger.

VI

ONE COUNTRY
TWO SYSTEMS

在"一国"的基础之上，
"两制"的关系应该也完全可以做到和谐相处、
相互促进。要把坚持"一国"原则和尊重"两制"差异、维
护中央权力 [...] 任何时候都不能偏废。
只有这样，"一国两制"这艘航船才能劈波斩浪、
行稳致远。

At no time should we focus only on one aspect to
the neglect of the other. Only in this way can we
ensure that the ship of "One Country, Two
Systems" will maintain a steady course and reach its
destination despite any rough seas.

When a boy becomes twenty years old, it's called coming of age. Today we celebrate the Adult Ceremony of Hong Kong Special Administrative Region. As the ancient saying goes, "Thrive like bamboo, prosper like pine."

Hong Kong is a pluralistic society. So it comes with no surprise that there are different views and even major differences of opinion on some specific issues. However, politicizing everything or deliberately creating differences and provoking confrontations will not resolve these problems. On the contrary, it will serve to hinder Hong Kong's economic and social development.

"One Country, Two Systems" is the best solution for Hong Kong issue left behind by the past. It is also the best institutional arrangement for maintaining long-term prosperity and stability after Hong Kong's return to the Mainland. It is feasible, achievable and popular.

The principle of "One Country, Two Systems" is a great Chinese invention and has gathered all schools of Chinese wisdom embracing diversity of mind and generosity of spirit.

At present, the practice of "One Country, Two Systems" in Hong Kong has encountered some new problems and new issues. Any action that jeopardizes the sovereignty of the Chinese state, challenges the authority of the central government and the authority of the Hong Kong Basic Law and uses Hong Kong to infiltrate and sabotage the Mainland touches the bottom line and cannot be tolerated on any account.

Our compatriots in Macau are masters of their own house entitled to broad freedoms and democratic rights in accordance with law. Macau enjoys orderly progress in democracy, fast economic growth, rising living standards, and social harmony and stability.

It is necessary to make long-term planning, seize the opportunity of the national efforts to comprehensively deepen reform, and promote appropriately diversified and sustainable economic development of Macau based on its positioning as a global tourism and leisure hub and a service platform for economic and trade cooperation between China and Portuguese-speaking countries.

Love for China and love for Macau have become

a prevalent value in Macau society.

VII

ONE CHINA

我们绝不允许任何人、任何组织、任何政党、在任何时候、以
任何形式、把任何一块中国领土从中国分裂出去，谁都不要指望我
们会吞下损害我国主权、安全、发展利益的苦果。
We absolutely will not allow anybody, any
organization, any political party, at any time and in
any form, to split any part of the Chinese territory.
Nobody should expect us to swallow the bitter fruits
that undermine the sovereignty, security and
development of our country.

We cannot lose even one inch of the territory left behind by our ancestors. What is other people's, we do not want at all.

Safeguarding national sovereignty and territorial integrity and realising the complete reunification of the country are the common aspirations of all the sons and daughters of the Chinese nation. All acts and tricks to split China are doomed to failure and will be condemned by the people and punished by history!

The Chinese people have a firm will, full confidence, and sufficient ability to frustrate all activities to split up the country! The Chinese people and the Chinese nation share a common belief that every inch of our great motherland's territory cannot possibly be separated from China!

The Chinese people share a common belief that it is never allowed and it is absolutely impossible to separate any inch of our great country's territory from China.

Safeguarding the interests of our Taiwan

compatriots and expanding their well-being is the mainland's oft-repeated pledge and solemn promise of the new leaders of China's Communist Party Central Committee.

We have the confidence and ability to keep a firm hold on the correct direction, work for the peaceful development of cross-Strait relations, and advance the process toward the peaceful reunification of China.

Once seeing through a long-term perspective and with a broad vision, compatriots from the two sides of the Strait would grasp the big picture of cross-Strait relations and overcome difficulties to push it forward.

Of course, we also are soberly aware that historical problems remain in cross-strait relations, and that there will be issues in the future that will require time, patience and joint efforts to resolve.

[We should] set our eyes in the future. The political differences between the Chinese mainland and Taiwan should eventually be solved step by step, and [we] cannot let these problems hand on from generation to generation.

We have the determination, the confidence, and the ability to defeat separatist attempts for "Taiwan independence" in any form.

A strong nation is the blessing for the siblings living on both sides of the Taiwan Strait. A weak nation is the disaster for the siblings living on both sides of the Taiwan Strait. Achieving the great rejuvenation of the Chinese nation is clearly connected to the destiny of the siblings living on both sides of the Taiwan Strait.

If the common political foundation on both sides of the Taiwan Strait is destroyed, then there is no solid base and the whole thing will shake and collapse.

The people know and understand quite well that both Kuomintang and Chinese Communist Party have contributed to the Cross-Strait Relations and its peaceful development, which has been written into history.

I am glad to see that five months after we established ties, the cooperation and exchanges between our two countries has proceeded in full speed which serves as a good beginning.[4]

4 [In June 2017 Panama announced that it was breaking ties with Taiwan to establish full diplomatic relations with China, the second-biggest user of the Panama Canal. Xi Jinping hails Panama leader as a hero for cutting links with Taiwan in favour of mainland China - South China Morning Post]

VIII

GOVERNANCE

治大国如烹小鲜。
Governing a big country
is like cooking a small dish.
Law is the very foundation of governance.[5]

Acting strongly according to the laws leads to strong and successful governance whereas acting weakly according to the laws leads to poor and unacceptable governance.[6]

Providing reward and penalty automatically, Fa strictly defines state functions through binding, general rules, removing from discussion what would otherwise only be opinion, and preventing conflicts of competencies, undue powers or profits. To this end, the legalist high officials focus solely on definition through calculation and the construction of objective models, judged solely by effectiveness. The Legalist school of philosophy emphasizes the need for order above all other human concerns and advocates a system of laws that rigidly prescribe punishments and rewards for specific behaviors. They underline the direction of all human activity toward the goal of increasing the power of the ruler and the state.]

[Arguing] whether the party is above the law or under the law is a political trap and an invalid argument. We will not give ambiguous answers to such a question.

The essence of the people's democracy is that the people get to discuss their own affairs.

Democracy is not an ornament. It is not used for decoration. It is used to solve the problems that the people want to solve.

The principal contradiction in the new era is the contradiction between unbalanced and inadequate development and the people's ever-growing needs for a better life.

We must show zero tolerance to these "three forces": terrorism, separatism and extremism. Violent terrorist activities must be stopped in an early stage and on a small scale or even wiped out before it has a chance to spread. With our iron fist we must deliver a devastating blow to destroy terrorism at a lightning speed.

We must have a profound understanding of the continuing, complex and sensitive nature of the struggle between separatism and anti-separatism in Xinjiang. Anti-violence and anti-terrorism cannot slow down at all. We must take resolute measures and firmly lay down the arrogance of the violent terrorists.

Just as one loves one's own eyes, one must love ethnic unity; just as one takes one's own livelihood seriously, one must take ethnic unity seriously.

The "great wall of iron" to safeguard national

unity, ethnic solidarity and social stability should be fortified in China's Xinjiang Uygur Autonomous Region.

We must resolutely guard against overseas infiltrations via religious means and prevent ideological infringement by extremists. We must give greater attention to religious affairs on the internet, and utilize it as a mean to promulgate the Party's idea and principle on religion, and spread the proper message on the issue.

Taking on responsibilities means fulfilling one's office diligently. Decisions and plans must be executed in full, and one must see things through from beginning to end, to ensure that no one simply goes through the motions or treats plans as a temporary measure, like a passing gust of wind.

Those who have never had power and those who are kept away from power tend to think everything associated with power is mysterious and unusual. But I looked under the surface of power, wreath, glory and applause and I saw the confinement as well as the reckless relationships. And so I have learnt to examine the entire picture of politics.

IX

INNOVATION
WITH CHINESE
CHARACTERISTICS

我们比历史上任何时期都更接近
中华民族伟大复兴的目标,
我们比历史上任何时期都更需要建设世界科技强国!
We are closer to the goal of the great
rejuvenation of the Chinese nation than any other
time in history. Our need to build a powerful
country of science and technology is more intense
than any other time in history!

The initiatives of innovation and development must be securely kept in our own hands.

Party leadership is the fundamental political guarantee of advances made in the cause of scientific innovation with Chinese characteristics.

Self-determination and innovation is the unavoidable path to climb to the world's top as a leading player in technology. We [should] hold innovative development tightly in our own hands. [We have to] put much effort in key areas where we are facing bottlenecks and make breakthroughs as soon as we can.

The core technologies are the core strength of our nation. We must make up our mind, maintain our perseverance and identify our focus in order to accelerate the breakthrough in the field of information core technologies.

When science and technology flourish, the nation will flourish, and strong science and technology lead to a strong country.

We are closer to the goal of the great rejuvenation of the Chinese nation than any other time in history. Our need to build a powerful country of science and technology is more intense than any other time in history.

We must fully understand that innovation is our primary driving force so that we can provide high-quality science and technology supplies and strive to support the construction of a modern economic system.

Technology is the key instrument of our country. Our nation depends on it, our enterprises rely on it to succeed, our people's lives count on it. If China wants to become stronger and the Chinese people want to live better, we must have robust science and technology.

We must aim at world-class cutting edge science and technology, lead the world's technological development, seize the opportunity to meet difficulties and build a strong country of world-class science and technology.

X

LAW & VIRTUE

深入实施公民道德建设工程，推进社会公德、职业道德、家庭美德、个人品德建设，激励人们向上向善、孝老爱亲，忠于祖国、忠于人民。

We will launch a civic morality campaign to raise public ethical standards, and enhance work ethics, family virtues, and personal integrity. We will encourage our people to strive for excellence and to develop stronger virtues, respect the elderly, love families, and be loyal to the country and the people.

Upholding the Party's leadership is fundamental to socialist rule of law, and is integral to our comprehensive efforts to advance the rule of law in China. (...) Upholding the Party's leadership is not an empty slogan but something that must be manifested in practice, through the Party's endeavors to lead legislation, ensure law enforcement, support the admiration of justice, and take the lead in abiding by the law.

We need to motivate the public to actively involve themselves in the practice of the rule of law; enable the people as a whole to become devoted advocates, conscientious observers, and resolute defenders of the socialist rule of law; and ensure that all share a common aspiration to respect the law, trust the law, observe the law, apply the law and defend the law.

The law enforcers must be loyal to the law.

We must integrate the rule of law with the rule of virtue.

The legal system of ancient China embodied a huge wealth of knowledge and wisdom, allowing to occupy a unique place among the major legal systems of the world.

Laws are ethics that have been written down, while are laws that we follow in our hearts. Both function to regulate social behavior and maintain social order.

Wherever offenders may flee, they will be brought back and brought to justice.

XI

FREEDOM OF SPEECH & HUMAN RIGHTS

自由是秩序的目的，秩序是自由的保障。
Freedom is what order is meant for,
and order is the guarantee of freedom.

We must never give those who maliciously attack the leadership of the Party, attack the socialist system, distort the party history and cite rumors free space and facilitate their need.

A handful of reactionary intellectuals are using the Internet to spread harmful attacks, slander and rumors against our Party's leadership, our socialist system and our state and must be seriously cracked down.

First, China doesn't export revolutions; second, China doesn't export hunger and poverty; third, China doesn't come and cause you headaches, what more is there to be said?

All work of the party's news and public opinion media must reflect the will of the party, mirror the views of the party, preserve the authority of the party, preserve the unity of the party, and achieve love of the Party, protection of the party and acting for the party. Media must maintain a high level of uniformity with the party in ideology, politics and action.

China attaches great importance to the protection of human rights. We insist on uniting universal human rights with the Chinese reality and we have found our own path to develop human rights suitable for the Chinese situation. Regarding human rights, I think the right decision should lie in the hand of the majority of our own people.

Universal values are a conspiracy for our enemies to sell lies to compete with our Party and to win our people's heart so that they can eventually overthrow the Chinese Communist Party. Tolerating them will irrefutably confuse our ideology and threaten the Party's ruling power.

"Happy National Day"

"Together we fulfill the Chinese dream"

"I give everything to our Party"

XII

CORRUPTION
& DISCIPLINE

纪律和规则对任何政党都是不可或缺的，
尤其是马克思主义政党。

Discipline and rule
are indispensable for political parties,
especially for Marxist parties.

No factions of self-interest are allowed in the Party, and those who form them actually violate political discipline. To prevent such phenomena from the outset, we need to promote the observance of political rules. Some officials group together as fellow townsmen or alumni. They hold regular gatherings, and rank themselves according to seniority as old-time graduates of the former Whampoa Military Academy did. Such activities, though seemingly casual, are not healthy. In reality, they have ulterior motives – their real intention is to form a kind of fraternity, in which members may support each other and collude when necessary. This is against Party rules. People should avoid such gatherings and dinners.

Be loyal to the Party, serve the people, act on laws and policies justly and keep strict discipline.

Happiness does not fall out of the blue and dreams will not come true by themselves. We need to be down-to-earth and work hard. We should uphold the idea that working hard is the most honorable, noblest, greatest and most beautiful virtue.

There is no such thing as "House of Cards". In our vigorous campaign against corruption during recent times, we have punished "tigers" as well as "flies". We have punished corrupt officials irrespective of ranking, in response to our people's demand. This has nothing to do with power struggle. It's nothing like what you see in House of Cards.

Seek good examples so as to become better but avoid bad examples as if facing enduring harm.

Fight tigers as well as flies.

Corruption could lead to the collapse of the Party and the downfall of the State.

To further promote anti-corruption efforts, we need to insist on the successful experiences gained through the Party's long-term anti-corruption practice. We need to actively draw on effective practices conducted by foreign countries around the world, and our own valuable heritage.

When promoting and assigning an official, the criteria should be his or her integrity and merit, not background, and whether he or she is suitable for the position.

Political integrity will be the foremost criterion for selecting officials. The outstanding problems in the party of impure thinking, impure politics, impure organization and impure work styles have yet to be fundamentally resolved.

XIII

ENVIRONMENT

宁肯不要钱，也不要污染。
We would rather give up on money
than giving in to pollution.

The Paris agreement is a milestone in the history of climate governance. We must ensure this endeavor is not derailed.

We should achieve the harmony between mankind and nature, the harmony between man and heaven. We should not try to conquer heaven.

Protect one's environment just like protecting one's eyes!

Lush mountain represents beauty. Blue sky represents happiness.

Ecological success means the success of Chinese civilization. Ecological failure means the failure of the Chinese civilization.

If you are kind to the environment, the environment is kind to you too. If you pollute the environment, the environment will one day betray you and take revenge mercilessly.

To survive, it's important to have gold mountains and silver mountains. However, lucid water and lush mountains make up the essential part of Chinese people's happiness that cannot be replaced by money.

We not only want to own lucid water and lush mountains, we also want to own gold and silver mountains. We choose lucid water and lush mountains above gold and silver. Most of all, lucid water and lush mountains are invaluable assets.

We vigorously promote the construction of an ecological civilization as well as strive to build a beautiful China so as to achieve the interminable advance of the Chinese nation.

Make our country and people see more blue sky, appreciate more green mountains, drink more clean water, and live in a more beautiful environment. We breathe new life into a new era of ecological civilization.

XIV

SOCIETY

最大限度增加和谐因素，
最大限度减少不和谐因素。[7]
Maximize the harmonious factors
and minimize the disharmonious factors.[7]

7 [*'The harmonious society'* 和谐社会 is a concept that was introduced by President Hu Jintao as a vision or objective for the country's future socioeconomic development. In the Chinese culture the two concepts, i.e. conflict versus harmony, prevailed. Subsequently, the Chinese state governance has been dominated by two schools of thoughts. The legalist school particularly focuses on conflict while Confucian school pays a great attention to promote harmony. The Legalists believe that political institutions should be modeled in response to the realities of human behavior and that human beings are inherently selfish and short-sighted. Contrary to the Confucians who trust that harmony can be assured through the recognition by the people of the virtue of their ruler, the Legalists believe social harmony can only be achieved through strong state control and absolute obedience to authority. Thus harmonious society is only possible when governed by absolute or omnipotent sovereign to control this state of insecurity. Confucians are mainly interested in how to bring about societal order that is called "harmony". Confucius believed that mankind would be in harmony with the universe if everyone understood their rank in society and were taught the proper behaviors of their rank. Similarly, he believed that "harmony" was threatened whenever people failed to act according to their prescribed roles. "A place for everyone and everyone in their place", "Respect my authority!" are the crucial ideas around which the Confucian harmony is designed. This hierarchy-oriented, status-centered nature was the *raison d'être* for Chairman Mao to fiercely reject Confucius as "spokesman of the decadent slave-owning aristocracy". Curiously, harmony is typically used as a verb by the Chinese. When something is "harmony-ed", it means the content is censored by the authority. One of the well-known example is the harmony-ed Winnie the Pooh, here on BBC News > ***bit.ly/PooBanned***]

We will unite the Chinese people of all ethnic groups and lead them to a decisive victory in building a moderately prosperous society in all respects and in the drive to secure the success of socialism with Chinese characteristics for a new era.

In 2020, we will establish a moderately prosperous society across all metrics. This is the society to be enjoyed by each and every one of us. On the march towards common prosperity, no one must be left behind. We will mobilize the whole Party and the whole country in a resolute push to deliver on our pledge and eradicate poverty in China.

Treat the elderly with true heart and true feeling.

Veteran cadres are an important resource for the party in governing and strengthening the country and an important force for promoting the great cause of socialism with Chinese characteristics.

I hope that the vast numbers of veteran cadres will cherish their glorious past, never forget their revolutionary aspirations, forever maintain the true political heart and continue to be an uncompromising supporter and exemplary practitioner of a thoroughgoing, hard rule of the Party.

Youth is the most sensitive barometer[8] of the times, whom bestows the responsibility of the times and to whom belongs the glory of the times.

8 [Propaganda in China today is much different than what it was from the 1950s to the 1970s. Every type of new media is used to propagate government messages and promote official viewpoints in the entertainment industry and educational system aiming at the country's youth. Textbooks are already being revised to include Xi's "Thought on Socialism with Chinese Characteristics in the New Era," and new research centers are being established at select universities. Most of all, interactive, playful, and trendy, this is what propaganda looks like today.

Expanded reading:

bit.ly/XiThoughtUni

http://bit.ly/XiatSchool
bit.ly/XiRap (link in Dutch) **]**

The youth must consciously practice the socialist core values.[9]

[9] **[** Socialist core values are 12 values, written in 24 Chinese characters, including the national values of prosperity, democracy, civility, and harmony; the social values of freedom, equality, justice, and the rule by law; and the individual values of patriotism, dedication, integrity and friendship.

国家层面的价值目标：富强、民主、文明、和谐社会层面的价值取向：自由、平等、公正、法治公民个人层面的价值准则：爱国、敬业、诚信、友善 **]**

The value orientation of the youth determines the value orientation of the future society. The youth is the stage of the formation and therefore it is very important to direct the foundation and development of the youth. This is like buttoning your shirt. If the first button goes wrong, the rest of the buttons will go wrong completely. The buttons of life should be fastened correctly from the beginning.

China will more actively implement the basic national policy of equality between men and women, give full play to the role of women as "half the sky", and support women in their efforts to build their own careers and realize their dreams and ideals.[10]

10 [Xi invoked the famous Mao Zedong's line from 1968: *"Dare to struggle, dare to win; women hold up half the sky."* 敢于斗争，敢于胜利，妇女能顶半边天。]

The majority of women should consciously shoulder the responsibility of respecting the elders, loving the young ones and educating their children, play a role in conserving and safeguarding family virtues, help the children form beautiful heart and soul, help them to grow up in a healthy way to become useful to our country and our people.

The majority of women should carry forward the fine Chinese tradition of hard working and self-improvement, pursue a positive, noble and civilized life, and support the formation of a good society.[11]

11 [Xi's words on the role of modern Chinese women have caused quite a stir on Weibo, the Chinese equivalent of Twitter. Social media comments wrote that the high-rank Party cadres are actually afraid that their sons aren't up for fair competition on the labor market, and on the policy level, Xi's traditional language would worm its way in harming and

discrediting young working women making a career. In recent years, a number of schools teaching "traditional feminine virtues" have sprung up nationwide. Read more on the contemporary "feminine virtues" teaching Chinese women four principles to stay at the bottom level that has been increasingly gaining popularity: *"Don't hit back when he beats you, don't say a word when he insults you, meekly submit to oppression and never ever ask for a divorce."* 打不还手，骂不还口，逆来顺受，绝不离婚 . Further reading: *"School teaching women housework and obedience forced to close in China"*
The Telegraph > *bit.ly/ObeySchool*]

To breed talents we must rely on education. Education means to cultivate the constructors and successors of socialism with Chinese characteristics instead of the bystanders and opponents.

XV

ECONOMY & INDUSTRY

任何否定、怀疑、动摇我国基本经济制度的言行都
不符合党和国家方针政策，都不要听、不要信！
所有民营企业和民营企业家完全可以吃下定心丸，
安心谋发展！

Any words and deeds that negate, doubt, or shake
China's basic economic system
are not in line with the principles and policies of our
Party and state.
Do not listen! Do not believe!

All private enterprises and private entrepreneurs can be completely reassured that they will have peace of mind to seek growth!

The economy is shifting from a high to a medium high rate of growth, from a growth model that emphasized scale and rate to one that emphasizes quality and efficiency.

The country's basic economic system was defined at the 15th CPC National Congress in 1997. It was pointed out emphatically at the congress that the private sector is an important component of China's market economy. The 16th CPC National Congress in 2002 decided to "consolidate and develop the public sector of the economy" and "encourage, support and guide the development of the private sector of the economy. (...) It was further noted at the 18th CPC National Congress in 2012 that China would "ensure that economic entities under all forms of ownership have equal access to factors of production in accordance with the law, compete on a level playing field and are protected by the law as equals.

China will continue to develop itself with its

door wide open. China will build a more investment-friendly environment that is aligned with international standards, more transparent and law-based and encourages competition and opposes monopoly. China will take tough law enforcement steps to strengthen protection of intellectual property rights and make IPR infringement even more costly. We encourage companies to maintain normal technological exchanges and cooperation, and will see to it that their lawful intellectual property rights are protected. China will also increase imports to promote balance of payment under the current account.

Strengthen the Party's leadership in all areas of our society, including foreign enterprises.

China's open door will not be closed, it will be only be opened wider.

State-owned enterprises with Chinese characteristics. "Chinese characteristics" means we must integrate the Party's leadership into every aspect of corporate governance. We make the state-owned enterprises bigger and stronger, but at the same time we establish Party organization in small enterprises and even private enterprises.

Strengthen the party's leading position in the enterprises, and some joint ventures will hand over major decisions to the Party organization.[12]

[12] [*"Foreign companies in China get a new partner: The Communist Party"* Business Standard > *bit.ly/ChinaNBP*

Also read three Chinese science institution recruiting for a president are opening search to foreigners. But said foreign scholars must have made an "in-depth study of Xi Jinping's socialist thought with Chinese characteristics in the new era". Link in Chinese: *bit.ly/XiforForeigners*]

The construction of economy is our Party's core work. Ideological work is an intensely crucial task of our Party's work.

Sink our teeth in the hard bone, show our courage and guts to press ahead and take reform forward.

China's aircraft industry has taken another step forward on the Long March. We must have our own commercial aircraft.

Development is always the key to solve any problem.

XVI

CULTURE AND ARTS

社会主义文艺，从本质上讲， 就是人民的文艺。
Socialist literature and art are, in essence, the
literature and art of the people.

Art and culture will emit the greatest positive
energy when the Marxist view of art and culture is
firmly established.

Our writers and artists must answer these questions: Who do we serve? Who do we rely on? Who am I?

There is no sustained inspiration or passion for art to be found in an ivory tower.

Literature and art will not hearten people to press on if they simply expose the darkness and account for the status quo without extolling brightness and ideals and offering moral guidance

To speak for the people, literature and art must follow the right path of serving the people and serving the socialist cause. (...) The people are the best connoisseurs and critics of literary and art works, and serving them is the duty of all writers and artists.

Contemporary Chinese values are those of socialism with Chinese characteristics. It indicates the direction where China's advanced culture moves forward.

Literature and art is an important cause of our Party and our people, and the literary and artistic front is the important front of our Party and our people.

Base entertainment is not the same as affable entertainment. Desire does not represent hope. Sensory distraction does not equal spiritual satisfaction. The fine quality in "quality art" lies in its ideological, artistic skills; everything is ceaselessly well-examined.

Literary and artistic workers should be ambitious.

In the field of creating literary and artistic works, there is a tendency to pursue quantity rather than quality. We see too many "plateaus" that lack of a "peak". Plagiarism, copying, stereotyped faker. The repetitive production for fast food consumption.

Literature and art cannot lose its course in the disorientating waves of market economy. It cannot move away its real purpose and from whom it is serving or else literature and art will have no vitality.

Your work praises patriotism. However, some spy dramas nowadays do not respect history, causing some harmful effects on the audience.

Some Chinese movie makers ignore the values they should promote.

XVII

INTERNET & BIG DATA

互联网可亡党亡国。
Internet can destroy our Party and our country.

Without web security there's no national security, there's no economic and social stability, and it's difficult to ensure the interests of the broader masses."

As in the real world, freedom and order are both necessary in cyberspace.

Cyberspace is not a place [that is] beyond the rule of law.

China is a firm defender of cyber security.

The Internet has become the main battlefield for the public opinion struggle.

We must build a nationwide integrated big data center.

Respect cyber sovereignty and carry forward the spirit of partnership.[13]

13 [*In December 2017, Xi spoke at the annual Beijing-sponsored World Internet Conference and reaffirmed "cyber sovereignty is key in China's vision of internet development". Already at the World Internet Conference 2015, Xi called for states to be allowed to set their own rules for cyberspace in their own countries. In other words, Xi appeared to be advocating for China's continued ability to limit its citizens' access to the Internet, and for a greatly reduced U.S. role in Internet operations and rule setting in the country. Read also "Man in China sentenced to five years' jail for running VPN" >* **bit.ly/VPNJail**

"Google plans to launch censored search engine in China" > **http://bit.ly/CensoredGoogle**]

Developing big data really makes sense.

We must pursue innovation-driven development, strengthen the cooperation in the frontier fields such as e-economy, artificial intelligence, nanotechnology and quantum computers and stimulate the technology of big data, cloud computing and smart cities in order to build the vastly connected digital Silk Road of the 21st century.

We must acutely understand the role of the

Internet in state administration and social governance. We should take the implementation of digital systems as well as the realization of a new type of smart city as our starting point and establish a national, integrated big data center through data centralization and sharing.

To achieve our goal, our online and offline life must form concentric circles. What are concentric circles? It means that under the leadership of our Party we mobilize the people of all nationalities and assemble the interest of all parts and layers so as to jointly push for the great rejuvenation of the Chinese nation that is the Chinese Dream.

Based on our specific needs, I believe that Internet public opinion should become the most important task of our propaganda and ideological work. Propaganda and ideological work is people's work. Where the people are is where we focus our work. China's netizens count nearly 600 million, mobile internet users count more than 460 million, of which microblog users have reached more than 300 million. We must face it and boost our power and thus lead the public opinion on the Internet instead of being marginalized.

Innovation cannot be given by others. Especially critical technologies and core technologies can only develop through our own hard work or else we are behind everyone else.

Robotics and intelligent manufacturing have been roped in as the top priority for Chinese science and tech innovation. We will hearten the research and development of industrial robotics and make the robotics and its products better in order to benefit the people.

Despite a failed deal, our friendship remains.[14]

14 [*About Mark Zuckerberg, who keeps a book by Xi Jinping on his desk - bit.ly/zuckerbook*]

XVIII

MEDIA

[党的新闻舆论媒体]都要增强看齐意识，
在思想上政治上行动上同党中央保持高度一致。
Media must maintain a high level of uniformity with
the party in ideology, politics and action.

All work of the party's news and public opinion media must reflect the will of the party, mirror the views of the party, preserve the authority of the party, preserve the unity of the party, and achieve love of the party, protection of the party and acting for the party.

Truthfulness is the life of journalism, and the facts must be reported based on the truth. While accurately reporting individual facts, journalists must also grasp and reflect the overall situation of an event from a broad view.

Officials should improve their ability to interact with the media and make good use of it to publicize their policies and ideas, understand grassroots opinions, uncover conflicts and problems, guide public feelings, mobilize the people and push forward work in real life

We do not need more praises and glorification. We have always welcomed objective report and useful suggestions.

Our plum blossom does not seek the viewer's

approval, leaving its pure fragrance to fill Heaven and Earth.[15]

15 [*The original quote is from a poem written by Wang Mian (14th century).*]

The media run by the Party and the government are the battlefield of propagandizing ideas of the Party and the government and must bear the Party's surname and follow the Party's rules.

Be the journalist our Party and people can trust.

We must follow the correct political direction and maintain a high degree of agreement with our Party and our central government. We must pursue Marxist journalism and defend the stand of our party and people. We must advocate socialism with Chinese characteristics and be a press worker with a firm political vision.

Western media wear colored glasses when looking at us. They usually misinterpret good things to be bad, leading the public opinion astray by making a fuss. Why should we be soft on them?

The West advertises their free press. The fact is

that they also have their own ideological bottom line, their own interests and political biases. There isn't any press that is completely independent.

XIX

INTERNATIONAL RELATIONS

我们不输入外国模式，也不输出中国模式，
不会要求别国复制中国的做法。
We neither 'import' foreign models
nor 'export' the Chinese Model.
We will not ask other countries
to 'copy' China's practices.

As only the wearer can know if the shoes fit him or not, only the people of the country have the right to talk about if the path of development suits them or not.

Together with all parties, China will work with greater efforts to build a lasting, peaceful, safe, prosperous, tolerant and clean and beautiful world that will last.

Work together to build a community with a shared future for mankind.

They may also choose to sit down quietly and drink tea while chatting about their lives.[16]

[16] [*This president Xi's quote is often used by Chinese websites promoting and selling Chinese tea.*]

Abandon the Cold War mentality and say no to zero-sum game.

Bosom friends make distance disappear.

As a Chinese saying goes: "Even mountains and seas cannot distance people with common aspirations."

China will always be a builder of world peace, a contributor to global development and a keeper of international order.

China is a peaceful, amiable, civilized lion.

Dare to pull our sword and strike to secure our interest.

China will actively take part in reforming and constructing the global governance system, and ensuring the world political and economic order develops in a more just and reasonable direction.

As a Chinese saying goes, "The sun and the moon shine in different ways, yet their brightness is just right for the day and the night respectively." It is precisely because of so many differences that the world has become such a diverse and colorful place, and that the need to broaden common ground and iron out differences has become so important.

China has always advocated that peoples of all countries have the right to choose their own development path. There is no universally accepted path in the entire world. If all things are the same, the development of all kinds of things will stop and the progress will end. Whether the development path suits the country, only its people have by far the most say.

All roads lead to Rome. No country should regard its own development path as number one, let alone impose its own development path on others.

We must also create more opportunities for the world by advancing China's development. We must explore the development laws of human society by deepening our own practices as well as share them with other countries in the world.

It makes clear that major country diplomacy with Chinese characteristics aims to foster a new type of international relations and build a community with a shared future for mankind.

The Chinese nation will become a proud and active member of the global community.

Openness brings progress while self-seclusion leaves one behind. China will not close its door to the world, and it will only become more and more open.

The Chinese people not only aspire for a good living for ourselves, but also hope people in other parts of the world lead a decent life. At present, people in certain countries and regions are still troubled by wars and turbulence; many are suffering from diseases and disasters. I sincerely hope the international community will make concerted effort, work together in the belief that mankind shares the same fate as a community, and build our planet into a more peaceful and prosperous place to live in.

Taiwan remains the most important, the most sensitive issue in Sino-American relation.

Delightful sceneries will not be hidden from our view, and all rivers flow eastward in the end.[17]

[17] [The original quote is from a poem by Xin Qiji (12th century)]

With good cooperation between China and the United States as starting point, the world will have a stable ballast layer. It's a booster for the world peace.

I think both sides [China and United States] should work hard to build a new type of relationship between big powers. The two sides should cooperate with each other for a win-win result in order to benefit people from the two countries and the world.

The Chinese people look to the US for support and coordination so that corrupt elements will be denied - an overseas safe haven.

Peaches and plums do not talk, yet a path is formed beneath them. These worthy fruits of cooperation across the Pacific Ocean speak eloquently to the vitality and potential of Sino-US relation.

The broad Pacific Ocean is vast enough to stomach both China and the United States.

China and the EU are both builders of world peace, contributors to global development and defenders of the international order.

Only those who habitually threaten others will look at everyone else as threats.

Russia and China are the most crucial, the most important strategic partners. To deepen the all-round strategic partnership between the two countries has top priority in the overall diplomacy as well as the foreign relations for both countries.

I think our personalities are quite similar.[19]

19 [(About **Vladimir Putin**)

here, an opinion article on Alzazeera, by Maria Repnikova about the differences between both > *bit.ly/XinotPutin*]

It is the highest-level, most profound and strategically most significant relationship between major countries in the world. President Putin and I both think that the China-Russia comprehensive strategic partnership is mature, firm and stable.

President Putin is the leader of a great country who is influential around the world. He is my best, most intimate friend.

A barefooted man is not afraid of the one who is wearing shoes.

(The man who has nothing fears nobody.)

Uncertain times give birth to sages while hardships give rise to a nation.

China and African countries have built our friendship through shared joys and sorrows. Our shared past of trials and tribulations must not be forgotten by us. China is committed to giving all-round support that leads to mutually beneficial cooperation between China and Africa. China has always followed the principle of "sincerity, real result, affinity and good faith".

We defend the correct understanding of integrity and selfish profit and assist Africa to build their own nests to attract their own phoenixes.

We help improve their ability to develop on their own terms and benefit the African people. Together we will fulfill our dreams of rejuvenation.

The Chinese Dream and the African Dream fit together and are perfectly compatible.

China and African countries are destined to be good friends, good brothers and good partners, and China-Africa cooperation stands as a fine example of South-South cooperation.

Developing a good relationship between China and Germany is like driving a car: one should look far enough ahead.

There are a few foreigners, with full bellies, who have nothing better to do than try to point fingers at our country.

XX

GLOBAL GOVERNANCE

要深度参与全球科技治理，
贡献中国智慧，着力推动构建人类命运共同体。
We must deeply participate in the global scientific
and technological governance by contributing
China's wisdom and striving to build a community
of shared destiny.

China stands for democracy in international relations and the equality of all countries, big or small.

Obviously, the current international order is not a perfect one. But as long as it is rule-based, aims to be equitable and pursues win-win outcomes as its goal, such an international order should not be discarded at will, still less should it be dismantled and rebuilt all over again.

The path, the theory, the system, and the culture of socialism with Chinese characteristics have kept developing, blazing a new trail for other developing countries to achieve modernization. It offers a new option for other countries and nations who want to speed up their development while preserving their independence; and it offers Chinese wisdom and a Chinese approach to solving the problems facing mankind.

As the world economy is going through profound transition and changes, only by opening themselves can different countries achieve mutual benefit, shared prosperity and sustainable development. This should be the right choice for all countries.

We BRICS countries should firmly promote an open world economy, be resolute in rejecting unilateralism and protectionism, promote trade and investment liberalization and facilitation, and jointly steer the global economy toward greater openness, inclusiveness, balanced growth and win-win outcomes for all.

We should ensure that economic globalization will deliver more benefits. We should help emerging markets and developing countries, African countries and the least developed countries in particular, fully involve themselves in international division of labor and share in the benefits of economic globalization.

Those who fail to keep abreast of the trend of the times will fall behind and become irrelevant. What we can and should do is to seize opportunities, increase input in innovation, focus on creating new areas of growth and replace old growth drivers with new ones.

When new rules are made on such issues as innovation, trade and investment and intellectual property protection or on new frontiers including cyberspace, outer space or the polar regions, we should make sure that the views of emerging markets and developing countries are heeded, their interests and demands are taken into consideration, and there are sufficient opportunities for their development.

China must uphold the protection of the country's sovereignty, security and development interests, proactively participate in and show the way in reform of the global governance system, creating an even better web of global partnership relationships.

[We will] lead the reform of the global governance system with the concepts of fairness and justice.

XXI

TRADE WAR

在西方的概念中，如果有人打了你的左脸，
你会把右脸也转过来给他打。但在中国的文化中，
我们通常都会以牙还牙。
In the West you have the notion that if somebody
hits you on the left cheek,
you turn the other cheek.
In our culture, we punch back.

A trade war should be rejected, because there will be no winner. Economic hegemony is even more objectionable, as it will undermine the collective interests of the international community; those who pursue this course will only end up hurting themselves.

The cold war and zero-sum mentality looks out of place in today's world. Arrogance or only focusing on one's own interests will get nowhere. Only peaceful development and cooperation can truly bring win-win or all-win results.

We must discard Cold War thinking, group confrontation; we object to acts of getting one's own absolute security at the cost of other countries' security.

We reject selfish, shortsighted, closed, narrow policies, (we) uphold World Trade Organization rules, support a multi-lateral trade system, and building an open world economy.

On the march toward common prosperity, no

one should be left behind.

In the time when economic growth is weak, trade protectionism, isolationism, and populism arise and world peace and development face increasing challenges. There is a saying, 'we must not forget pain when the wound has healed.

The international financial crisis had happened just a few years ago. Lessons have yet to be learnt. We have not fully recovered. We believe that at this moment in time we should not start fighting each other. We should work together to bake a bigger cake.

Abandon those Cold War mentalities and zero sum games. We need to focus on win-win cooperation to build a new type of international relations.

China must have the courage to swim in the vast ocean of the global market. China took a brave step to embrace the global market.

XXII

WAR & DEFENSE

我们不惹事，但也不怕事。
We do not want to introduce trouble
but we are not afraid to get involved in trouble.

We strive to build a people's army that listens to our Party's order, can fight to win and forge exemplary conduct.

The People's Liberation Army must follow the absolute leadership of our Party.

Ideological work within the military should be strengthened and combat capability should be regarded as the criterion for military building.

The Chinese dream is not only a dream about a strong nation but also about a strong army. If we want to achieve the great rejuvenation of the Chinese nation, we must uphold the union of a rich country and a great army and strive to secure our national defense and bolster a well-built army.

The most important matter of a nation is nothing but the military.[20]

[20] [*Operation Red Sea*, the latest Chinese movie blockbuster, which was partly inspired by a Chinese military evacuation mission carried out in Yemen nearly three years ago is currently the fourth highest-grossing mainland Chinese film

Why must we stand firm on the Party's leadership over the military? Because that's the lesson from the collapse of the Soviet Union. In Soviet Union, where the military was depoliticized, separated from the Party and nationalized, the Party was disarmed. When the country came to crisis point, a big party was gone just like that. Proportionally, the Soviet Communist Party had more members than we (Communist Party of China) do, but nobody was man enough to stand up and resist.

It makes clear that the Party's goal of building a strong military in the new era is to build the people's forces into a world-class army that obey the Party's order, can fight to win, and maintain excellent conduct.

There is no such thing as the so-called Thucydides trap in the world. But should major countries time and again make those strategic mistakes of miscalculation, they might create such traps for themselves.

The People's Liberation Army is the people's army. All its officers, men and women must bear in mind their responsibility of serving the people whole-heartedly, faithfully fulfil the sacred duty of protecting the nation's security and people's well-being, and carry out the noble mission of upholding world peace.

If a soldier does not practice during peaceful times, he cannot fight the enemies in the war.[21]

21 [The quote is originally from Deng Xi Zi by Deng Xi (6 century BC). Deng Xi belongs to the Legalist School that emphasizes the need for order above all other human concerns. The political doctrine propagates total political control of the society, which must be maintained through brutal physical torture.]

The fundamental rule of commanding an army is consistency in thinking and action.

Once the military falls behind, its consequence on national security will be fatal. I often study the modern Chinese history. I feel deep pain whenever I read the tragic records of our country being beaten (by foreigners)!

When you are able to fight a war, then you can stop going to war. When you are ready for war, then you may not have to join the war. The more you cannot fight a war, the more likely you will be beaten. This is the dialectics of war and peace.

If our army is not reformed, we can never fight to win.

What I worry about the most is whether our army can abide by the absolute leadership of the Party when the Party and the people need us, whether we can go to the battle and win, whether the commanders can lead their troops to fight and keep control?

Our armed forces must prepare for war. The Chinese Military Committee (CMS) must understand how to fight a war and be skilled strategists and commanders. The work of the CMC is to put emphasis from the very beginning on fighting and winning a war.

in **Djibouti** (First Chinese overseas military base)

XXIII

ONE BELT
ONE ROAD

"一带一路"是开放的，源于古丝绸之路但不限于古丝绸之路，地域范围上东牵亚太经济圈，西接欧洲经济圈，是穿越非洲、环连亚欧的广阔朋友圈，所有感兴趣的国家都可以添加进入朋友圈。

China's Belt and Road Initiative is based on the historic roots of the Silk Road, it focuses on Asia, Europe and African continents, and is open to all friends.

Let more countries board the high-speed train through China's breakneck development.

The Belt and Road Initiative, guided by the principle of seeking shared benefits through extensive consultation and joint contribution, originated in China but belongs to the world. It is our sincere hope that other BRICS countries, African countries and other emerging markets and developing countries will forge strong partnerships with this initiative so that its benefits will reach more countries and their peoples.

We should guide economic globalization, cushion its negative impact and deliver its benefits to all countries.

We intend to build "One Belt and One Road" into a path of peace, a path of prosperity, a path of openness, a path of innovation and civilization.

Belt and Road Initiative has garnered great support from the Arab world and China stands ready to work with Arab states on the initiative. Arab states are natural partners of China.

History is the best teacher.

We will not follow the old way of geopolitical games during the push for the Belt and Road Initiative, but create a new model of win-win and cooperation. It will not form a small group undermining stability, but is set to build a big family with harmonious co-existence.

Swan geese are able to fly far and safely through winds and storms because they move in flocks and help each other as a team.

A country's opening-up is like the creation of butterfly from cocoon. It brings rebirth with short-term pain. We must orient the construction of Belt and Road Initiative on opening-up and try to solve problems concerning economic growth and balance.

Countries have the right to development, but they should view their own interests in the broader context. And refrain from pursuing their own interests at the expense of others.

We are living in a world with constant

challenges: The world economy needs new growth drivers, its development needs to be more balanced and universal, the wealth gap should be narrowed, while some regions are plagued with turbulence and terrorism. Peace, development and governance are challenges for all human beings.

XXI

SPACE

飞天梦是强国梦的重要组成部分。
The space dream is part of the dream
to make China stronger.

We must make every effort to advance the transformation of the armed forces, speed up the development of new types of combat forces and speed up its integration into the joint operation system of the entire army so that we can face any war and win any war.

We should cherish the dream of space superpower, make our mission even stronger, fortify the technological innovation and creativitythrough practice, and constantly boost China's ambition to conquer the space.

Exploring the vast universe, developing space programs and becoming an aerospace power have always been the dream we've been striving for.

Developing the space program and turning the country into a space power is the space dream that we have continuously pursued.

Seize the strategic opportunity and keep innovating to make a greater contribution to the country's overall growth and the welfare of mankind.

As we made 'Yutu' lay its prints on the moon, we also imprinted the extraordinary creativity of the Chinese nation onto the history of the human civilization.

The universe is vast and exploration of it will never end.

XXII

SOFT POWER[22]

中华优秀传统文化是我们最深厚的文化软实力。
也是中国特色社会主义植根的文化沃土。
The outstanding Chinese culture
is our most profound soft power.
It is also the fertile cultural ground where
socialism with Chinese characteristics is rooted.

22 ["Soft power", 软实力, a term coined by Harvard University scholar Joseph S. Nye Jr. in 1990, is the means by which a country gets other countries to "want what it wants". Nye emphasized that a country's perceived legitimacy, attractiveness of ideology and culture, and societal norms play an important role in shaping international politics. Chinese officials and academics expressed the importance of China's culture in the 1990s and early 2000s, but soft power was explicitly referenced in national government policy for the first time at the Seventeenth National Congress of the Chinese Communist Party in 2007. Former Chinese President Hu Jintao said, "The great rejuvenation of the Chinese nation will definitely be accompanied by the thriving of Chinese culture". This formulation, tying culture to the country's place on the world's stage, echoed other core principles from Chinese leadership, such as China's "peaceful rise" and its vision of a "harmonious society". These ideas intended to counter narratives from the West that China's emergence was a threat to the existing international order. Under Xi's leadership, China has pushed the notions of the "Chinese Dream" and "China Model" without providing clear definitions. However, contrary to the "bottom-up" approach, Chinese Communist Party believes in the top level design (顶层设计). Especially in Xi Jinping's China, it's all about "harmonious society" achieved through control which rejects and disallows bottom-up cultural influences. Most recently in his 19th Party Congress speech, Xi mentions the need to "implement the system of responsibility

for ideological work," a phrase that has traditionally implied deploying citizens to monitor one another. Regulations related to the new Cybersecurity Law that entered into force in June 2017 include provisions to encourage self-censorship. Just in October, the Party issued new rules that require social media and news applications to conduct regular self-assessments to ensure they are not hosting any undesirable content.

To coin a concept more accurate in describing ongoing Chinese efforts at expanding global influence while covertly exerting its own authoritarian sway, Jessica Ludwig and Christopher Walker fashioned the new term sharp power".

Expanded read: "China's secret 'magic weapon' for global soft power" in Democracy Digest > *bit.ly/ChinaMagic/* **]**

Many ideas and ethics drawn directly from the outstanding Chinese tradition hold their never-fading values both in the past and present. "Unlock the bounds of one's own life with the rules of the ancients". We must inherit and carry forward the outstanding Chinese traditional culture under the conditions of the new era in order to accomplish the creative transformation and innovative development of the Chinese culture.

We should take good care of our propaganda work and try innovative ways of propaganda abroad. We strive to create new expressions that integrate new ideas and new fields both at home and overseas and publicize good stories about China and broadcast a good Chinese voice.

Every novel, essay, painting, poem, photo, film, TV drama or musical piece offers a unique perspective on China for people in other countries, inviting, enticing and·impressing them in its own way. (…) You are expected to promote splendid Chinese arts globally, introduce foreign audiences to the charm of Chinese culture, and in the course help them develop a better understanding of it.

To promote China's soft power, we must strive to consolidate the foundation of our national soft power.

The Socialist Core Values[23] are the soul of cultural soft power and the focus of building Chinese cultural soft power.

[23] [The 12 Socialist Core Values, written in 24 Chinese characters: 富强(prosperity), 民主(democracy), 文明(civility), 和谐 (harmony), 自由 (freedom), 平等(equality), 公正 (justice), 法治 (the rule of law), 爱国(patriotism), 敬业 (dedication), 诚信(integrity), 友善(friendship).]

To enhance our cultural soft power, we must make an effort to improve our voice in the international communities and strengthen our capacity of amplifying worldwide communication.

Guide the Chinese people to enhance their honor and pride of being Chinese.

Improving the country's cultural soft power is a major strategic task for our party and our country.

The Chinese TV drama "Good Age for the Daughter-in-Law" was aired in Tanzania, so now the Tanzanian people understand the emotions of the Chinese people. China and Africa share an unforced familiarity and closeness. Life is good because people value one another.

The Korean TV series "My Love From the Star" is very popular with the young people in China. The Chinese people and the Korean people are also deepening and extending their cultural understanding for each other.

XXIII

TOILET REVOLUTION

坚持不懈推进"厕所革命"，
努力补齐影响群众生活品质短板。
We will unswervingly push forward
the "toilet revolution" and work hard to fill in the
shortcomings that affect the
quality of life of the masses.

The toilet issue is no trivial matter. It is an important aspect of the construction of urban and rural civilization. We should focus not only on the tourist places and cities but also the countryside. This effort should be pushed forward as a concrete project of the rejuvenation strategy for the rural area.

XXIV

FORMER LEADERS

毛泽东同志属于中国，也属于世界。
Comrade Mao Zedong belongs to China, but he
belongs to the world as well.

The development of our Party in all domains since the reform and openness policy for the past 30 years has been carried out according to the great construction plan of our Party, which was successfully conceived by the first generation of the communists of the central government under the core leadership of Comrade Mao Zedong.

As a scientific system, Mao Zedong Thought includes both his correct analysis of the New Democratic Movement and his correct view on building and fashioning socialism.

Comrade Mao Zedong led our Party through hard-wearing quests, which resulted in significant ideological achievements. This is not only the valuable asset of our Party but also the key inspiration for the theoretical framework of socialism with Chinese characteristics.

We must dig deep into the relationship between the theoretical framework of socialism with Chinese characteristics and the study of Marxism, Leninism, particularly Mao Zedong Thought.

Just imagine how our party could be tenable if we abandoned [the spirit] of Comrade Mao Zedong. Our socialistic system, the whole country would fall into chaos.

Comrade Deng Xiaoping has been lauded as a highly esteemed, exceptional leader by the entire Party, the entire army and the Chinese people of all nationalities, as well as a great Marxists, a great proletarian revolutionary, politician, military, diplomat. He was a tried and tested communist fighter, the chief architect of China's socialist reform and opening up policy and the country's modernization, the pioneer of the socialism with Chinese characteristics, and the founder of Deng Xiaoping Theory.

XXV

SPIRITUALITY

头上三尺有神明，一定要有敬畏之心
There are gods watching us from above.
We must have awe of them.
There is great wisdom in Buddhism about being
a human and doing good work.

Be reliable in politics, be accomplished in religion, be convincing in moral qualities and play a key role at the crucial moment. [24]

[24] [China's Communists were not always antagonistic toward religion. Before winning the civil war in 1949, the party found refuge in China's northwest. Its numbers reduced by disease and attacks, the Party needed local allies, such as Tibetan Buddhists and Hui Muslims, and pious Chinese farmers. So the party took a pragmatic approach, basically leaving religion alone as long as it didn't challenge party rule. This changed in the late 1950's during the last 20 years of Mao's life. According to WikiLeaks, as a young man Xi *"displayed a fascination with Buddhist martial arts, qigong and other mystical powers said to aid health, as well as with Buddhist sacred sites"*. Today, as the country's leader, Xi Jinping is designing a template for the mixing of faith and politics — a re-imagined political-religious state that once ruled the Chinese empire. In 2016, Master Chin Kung, a Buddhist Monk who is well known for using modern technology to spread the Buddha's teachings made one of his popular Buddhist teaching videos, in which he explained that President Xi Jinping is bodhisattva incarnation and because of him the entire world has entered a golden age.]

If the people have faith, the nation has hope,

and the country has strength.

There is a saying in our country: Become Buddha looking at the bare wall. This is the way to achieve transcendence.

The value and significance of Famen Temple is not only to be appreciated as cultural relics, but also to resurrect its intrinsic spiritual values.

The World Buddhist Forum is a great event for the Buddhist world, and it is also a major event in the religious work in our country. The participation of the Panchen Lama in the first World Buddhist Forum will surely further the friendly exchanges between the religious circles in China and foreign countries. I welcome the 11th Panchen to visit Zhejiang more often in the future and continue to advance the close relationship between Chinese and Tibetan peoples as well as the Buddhist communities.

I hope that the majority of religious figures will carry forward the excellent tradition of Tibetan Buddhism and patriotism, continue to strengthen self-cultivation, actively undertake social responsibilities, consciously safeguard the unity of our motherland and the unity of Chinese nationalities, and make positive contributions for

Tibet to achieve the goal of building a moderately prosperous society in an all-round way.

XXVI

UPCLOSE & PERSONAL

我最大的爱好就是读书，读书是我的生活方式。
My favorite hobby is reading.
It is part of my life.

I particularly like Hollywood World War II movies, and I also hope the United States continues making such productions. Hollywood can make this kind of movies very well. The scenes are vast and very realistic. In American movies, justice is usually served, which shows the Americans have clear values. They can clearly tell good from bad.

Everybody has his own ideal, his own pursuit and his own dreams.

I have watch Deer Hunter and The French Lieutenant's Woman starred by Meryl Streep, and Godfather.[25]

[25] [It is said that "The Godfather" has served as Xi Jinping's political education. Coppola's masterpiece has had no less influence on him than Comprehensive Mirror in Aid of Governance (1804) and Chairman Mao's Selected Works. In China's seventies, 'The Godfather' could not be viewed publicly and Xi must have watched the movie classic through internal circulation serving the Party's top echelons. It made a great impression on the young man, apparently. The New York Times wrote: "The president of China, Xi Jinping, has admitted to watching "The Godfather", and this week he proved he could be a shrewd student of one of that film's themes: the

I watched Dangal, and liked it.

I'm an enthusiast of sports like swimming and mountain climbing.

I am a soccer fan. The Chinese soccer team has been working really hard, but we have only once broken into the World Cup Championship. The man behind this historical moment is Milutinovic, who was also the Mexican national team coach.

APPENDIXES

Xi Dada
Loves Peng Mama[26]

China produced a Xi Dada,
He dares to fight the tigers.
Not afraid of heaven, not afraid of earth,
Dreamers all look to him!

China also has a Peng Mama,
Give her the most beautiful flowers.
Protect and bless her,
Flourishing family, flourishing country, flourishing
under heaven!

Xi Dada loves Peng Mama,
This sort of love is legendary,
Peng Mama loves Xi Dada,
The realm with love is the strongest!

Men should study Xi Dada,
Women should study Peng Mama,
Love like they do,
Love can warm everyone!

Men should study Xi Dada,
Women should study Peng Mama,
Love like they do,
People with love can win everything!

Brave love is called Xi Dada loves Peng Mama,
Together, he's always smiling happily at her.
Brave love is called Peng Mama loves Xi Dada,
Hand in hand, her smile is the most beautiful flower.

26 [Xi Dada Loves Peng Mama is a contemporary pop song created by a group of musicians from Henan province. They have reportedly worked for 2 hours on the song. On 18 November 2014, before midnight, they uploaded the song to the Internet. On 23 November it received 22 million hits and went viral. The lyricist, Song Zhigang is well known for his work hugely popular in karaoke halls and long-distance buses. Xi Jinping is the first communist leader who revolutionized the public image of China. As a policy the country has borrowed Western codes of political branding marketing based on a strong personification and emotionalisation of the discourse. In this "soft power" model, the wife plays an important role and helps her husband to attract public attention. China thus puts a strong spotlight on the first couple with Xi's wife Peng Liyuan next to him. Being familiar with limelight and taking on the role of beloved household name both domestically and internationally, Peng engagingly fulfills her tasks. Peng holds the rank of PLA major general and as an army singer she is best known for her stirring renditions of patriotic odes, often dressed in green military uniform. The pop song that has been promoted by state-run media sets the Middle Kingdom's contemporary moral standards: "Men should learn from Xi and women should learn from Peng".
here > *bit.ly/XilovesPeng* **]**

General Secretary, My Eyes Follow in Your Wake[27]

An ode to General Secretary Xi Jinping

by Xinhua State News Agency's

deputy editor

Pu Zhuozi

[February 19, 2016]

On this occasion, the thunderous applause
Drowns out the traffic along the ancient Xuanwumen
Gate
Today, the distance is finally closed
We listen to your fatherly earnest words and wishes
You smile and cup your hands in greeting: "I wish you all
A happy New Year, and divine wishes for the Year of the
Monkey!"

General Secretary, my eyes follow in your wake
And in these eyes, my verse takes shape
My cellphone grows hot as my fingers write

But for so long this poem has been brewing
It gnashes at my guts
It clinches my veins and nerves

It pitches on the Yellow River and the Yangtze Water
It races along the Great Wall
It joins the camel bells of the One Belt and One Road

And the mighty wind of the high-speed rail

Hehe! Right now
There is no starry night I am so familiar with whenever I
write poems
I can see light all dazzling and bright
Outside our building
But I can feel my verse soaring and dancing through my
spine and lungs

General Secretary, my eyes follow in your wake
Today there are loads of greetings to you
Today my poem is tearing my chest open
General Secretary, my eyes follow in your wake
You tread steadily forward raising your head
At Xinhua News Agency we will continue raising our
voice
Dashing toward modest prosperity
Getting closer to the Chinese Dream
We will face trials and specters on our journey
But we will keep calm, just like this afternoon
Smog shall not confuse our lucid mind!

General Secretary, my eyes follow in your wake
The admiring eyes of mine
and countless Xinhua people

27 [Transforming the country's head of state into
the object of public desire is not new to China.
Surfing on the current trend and intensifying it,
China Central Television (CCTV) recently broadcast
the show "Trust in China", in which a Chinese
actress tearfully cited a love letter written to
Chairman Mao Zedong decades ago.
here > *bit.ly/maoloveletter*]

ORIGINAL PHOTO [*Epoch Times*]

七律·军民情

挽住云河洗天青，
闽山闽水物华新。
小梅正吐黄金蕊，
老榕先掬碧玉心。
君驭南风冬亦暖，
我临东海情同深。
难得举城作一庆，
爱我人民爱我军。

CHAIRMAN'S POEM[28]

The military and the civilian
I embrace the river of clouds and cleanse the sparkling sky,
Watching the Min landscape parading our new China.
The young plum shows the gold-colored fluffy heart,
While the old Banyan tree reveals its jade-green spirit.
You ride on the southern wind that warms our cold winter,
While I face the eastern sea that deepens our spring lake.
This is a rare celebration where the entire community gathers
To love our people and our army.

[28] [In January 1991, the first national Support Military Families Conference since the founding of PRC was held in Fuzhou. Xi was Fuzhou

Municipal Party Committee Secretary and wrote this poem on the occasion, which was published in the Fujian Daily on January 13, 1991. Xi commented at the time: *"I have an indissoluble bond with the military. I feel deeply for them. I have been taught a lot about the history of our army in my childhood and have witnessed the grace of many military leaders from older generations. Ever since my teenage years, I have developed a genuine devotion to our army. I myself have worked in the army for several years, and I have always paid attention to the construction of our armed forces even after I left".*]

Tell China's story well, spread China's voice well. Let the world know a three-dimensional, colorful China.

讲好中国故事、传播好中国声音、
阐发中国精神、展现中国风貌。

Xi Jinping
习近平

If one day China should change her color
and turn into a superpower, if she too should
play the tyrant in the world, and everywhere
subject others to her bullying, aggression and
exploitation, the people of the world should
identify her as social-imperialism, expose it,
oppose it and work together with the Chinese
people
to overthrow it.

如果中国有朝一日变了颜色，变成一个超 级
大国，也在世界上称王称霸，到处欺负人家，侵略
人家，剥削人家，那么，世界人民就应当给中国戴
上一顶社会帝国主义的帽子，就应当揭露它，反对
它，并且同中国人民一道，打倒它。

Deng Xiaoping (邓小平) in a speech at the United Nations
April 10, 1974

Made in the USA
Middletown, DE
13 June 2019